4149

JESUS, BE IN MY CHRISTMAS

Other books by Sarah Hornsby

At the Name of Jesus
Who I Am in Jesus
The Fruit of the Spirit
Standing Firm in Jesus
Jesus, Be in Me
Getting to Know Jesus from A to Z
Nicaraguense

JESUS, BE IN MY CHRISTMAS

SARAH HORNSBY

√ chosen books

FLEMING H. REVELL COMPANY
TARRYTOWN, NEW YORK

Unless noted otherwise, Scripture texts are from the Holy Bible, New International Version, copyright © 1973, 1978, 1984 International Bible Society. Used by permission of Zondervan Bible Publishers.
Scripture quotations identified KJV are from the King James Version of the Bible.

Library of Congress Cataloging-in-Publication Data

Hornsby, Sarah.
    Jesus, be in my Christmas / Sarah Hornsby.
        p.   cm.
    ISBN 0-8007-9203-3
    1. Advent—Prayer-books and devotions—English.   2. Christmas—
Prayer-books and devotions—English.   I. Title.
BV40.H66   1992
242'.33—dc20   92-12740
                                                                              CIP

A Chosen book
Copyright © 1992 by Sarah Hornsby

Chosen Books Publishing Company, Ltd.
Published by
Fleming H. Revell Company
Tarrytown, New York
Printed in the United States of America

To my mother,
my faithful encourager,
Lutitia Elizabeth Toole Anderson

"As soon as the sound of your greeting reached my ears, the baby in my womb leaped for joy. Blessed is she who has believed that what the Lord has said to her will be accomplished!"

Luke 1:44–45

Acknowledgments

Special thanks to:
Chosen Books editors Jane Campbell and Ann McMath
My husband, Jim, for his patience
My son James' thoughtful critiques
And to the Nicaraguan children in my kids' club with
whom I exchanged flowers they had drawn for stickers:
Guillermo, Ilenia, Heidi, Claudia, Suleika, Fatima, Jose
Adrian, to name only a few.

Introduction

Advent is a time of wonder, of beginnings, of preparation. Advent is a wreath of pungent evergreens with candles glowing, reflecting on familiar faces, bringing a holy light to the ordinary. Advent is focus on faith that God comes among us bearing gifts through us.

Advent is God's gift of Jesus, His presence in the eternal wonder of birth. He is the best gift we can receive.

Advent is a time of nostalgia, of remembering "Christmas Past" and the stories of parents and grandparents of simpler times. My daddy told frequently of his delight as a child on Christmas morning to find in his handknit sock an orange, an apple and a stick of peppermint, prized because they were not often available on the farm in northern Illinois. This Advent study, asking Jesus to be in me at Christmas, has caused the memories to flame brighter and the meaning of the season to burst forth with greater significance for daily living.

Advent is a lonely time of stress and confusion for many in our Western culture. "Christmas Present" has become a glitzy grabbing for artificial joy in getting and giving things instead of the simplicity of God's gift of Himself.

As I wrote and drew these pages in our tropical town, nestled in the mountains of northern Nicaragua, it was easy to picture the palm trees, the hills of Nazareth and Bethlehem, the little houses huddled together for protection against bandits, the donkeys and chickens. Only when friends from Americus, Georgia, sent a packet of old Christmas cards for my kids' club did I remember to put snow in the drawings and boots and warm woolen scarves.

As I wrote, listening to Mary and Joseph and the angels, to the warning of a sword piercing, to the threat of an evil king killing little babies, I realized that the Christmas story is far more than a sweet thought, a tender, sentimental moment. Like the angels who still come through the cloven skies, God still penetrates our real worlds of Israel, of Nicaragua, of the United States today with the reality of His living Son, Jesus.

This book invites Him into my everyday world and yours. Jesus, be in my Christmas. . . .

Sarah Hornsby
Due West, South Carolina
October 28, 1991

To the reader:

Since Advent begins four Sundays before Christmas Day, its length can vary each year from 22 to 28 days. This book features two entries per day for 28 days, and can thus be adapted accordingly to an Advent season of any length.

Jesus, Be in My
Christmas

Jesus, Be in My Dreams

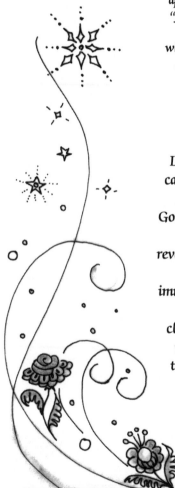

*This is how the birth of Jesus Christ
came about. . . . An angel of the Lord
appeared to [Joseph] in a dream and said,
"Joseph son of David, do not be afraid to
take Mary home as your wife, because
what is conceived in her is from the Holy
Spirit. She will give birth to a son, and
you are to give him the name Jesus,
because he will save his people
from their sins."*
Matthew 1:18–21

Like Joseph of Genesis, Joseph the
carpenter of Nazareth had a significant dream, a dream inspired by
God. His dream warned, instructed,
encouraged, enabled. God was
revealing His plan, choosing human
beings for divine tasks that had
immediate and eternal implications.
I need to keep my channels
clear, guarding what goes into my
mind, what I read, watch, listen
to. Even what I eat or when I go

to bed with unresolved
anger affects my
dreams. I want to hear
when God would speak
and direct me.

Father God, some of
my dreams are fanta-
sies, totally unrealistic.
Other dreams are nightmares
of horror. Enter all my dreams with
Your light. Illumine and guide me in
this Christmas season with dreams You
inspire. Jesus, be in my dreams.

"In the last days, God says, I will pour out my
Spirit on all people. Your sons and daughters will
prophesy, your young men will see visions, your
old men will dream dreams."

Acts 2:17–18

Jesus, Be in My Listening

The Sovereign Lord has given me an instructed tongue, to know the word that sustains the weary. He wakens me morning by morning, wakens my ear to listen like one being taught.
Isaiah 50:4

In the Christmas story, God spoke to Zechariah through an angel in the Temple; to Elizabeth through her husband; to Mary in her home; to Joseph in a dream; to the unborn child, John the Baptist, through Mary's greeting. To each of these simple Jewish folk, God brought unexpected news that utterly transformed their lives, fulfilling God's purposes in history. Like Anna and Simeon they were waiting, watching, listening for the Messiah. He came through them.

If I listen, God speaks daily to me, making the most ordinary circumstances profoundly holy. God speaks through words of wisdom, words of Scripture or song, through intuitive insight. God speaks through nature, events, friends, children, husbands/wives, through the sacraments. God even speaks through

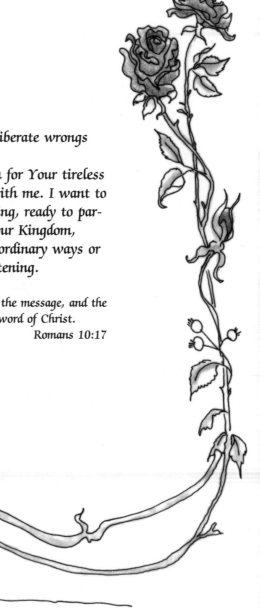

mistakes and through deliberate wrongs others do to me.

Father God, thank You for Your tireless efforts to communicate with me. I want to be open, available, listening, ready to participate in bringing in Your Kingdom, whether in small, quiet, ordinary ways or great. Jesus, be in my listening.

. . . Faith comes from hearing the message, and the message is heard through the word of Christ.

Romans 10:17

Jesus, Be in My Meditation

In the sixth month, God sent the angel Gabriel to Nazareth, a town in Galilee, to a virgin pledged to be married to a man named Joseph, a descendant of David. The virgin's name was Mary. The angel went to her and said, "Greetings, you who are highly favored! The Lord is with you."

Luke 1:26–28

God wants to communicate with us, make His will known. One way God touches me is through His messengers, the angels. Sometimes an angel appears to be a quite ordinary human being, but later, upon reflection, I realize that possibly this was one of God's guardian spirits. Sometimes things happen that cannot be explained logically. Unseen hands have been at work doing good, the natural touched by the supernatural.

For Mary, the angel's appearance was direct with a clear message of blessing, though to become pregnant outside of marriage would not seem to be good news!

Father God, no matter what message You have for me, I want to receive it. I want Your Holy Spirit's power to touch me. "May it be to me as You have said." Jesus, be in my meditation.

May the words of my mouth and the meditation of my heart be pleasing in your sight, O Lord, my Rock and my Redeemer.

Psalm 19:14

Jesus, Be in My Guidance

". . . When he, the Spirit of truth,
comes, he will guide you into all truth.
He will not speak on his own; he will
speak only what he hears, and he will tell
you what is yet to come."
John 16:13

It comes as a breath of fresh air to
know that the holy God wants to
communicate with me. God sent
Jesus, God in human flesh and
blood, to personally reveal the tender toughness of His love. Then
Jesus promised to send His Holy
Spirit, who is continually with
God and knows God's mind and
heart. In the same instant He
knows my mind and heart. The
Holy Spirit is expert in
communicating
and guiding.

The Holy Spirit impregnated
Mary and wants to fill me with
His power, enabling me to do
God's will, step by step in the
path Jesus walked.

Come, Holy Spirit, who guides into
all truth. Come, Holy Spirit, who con-
victs of all sin. Come, Holy Spirit,
Comforter, Counselor. Come, Holy
Spirit, whose prayers are God's perfect
will. Come, Holy Spirit. Whether with
groaning travail or with dancing joy,
come! Jesus, be in my guidance.

Let the wise listen and add to their learning,
and let the discerning get guidance.

Proverbs 1:5

Jesus, Be in My Expectation

"As soon as the sound of your greeting reached my ears, the baby in my womb leaped for joy. Blessed is she who has believed that what the Lord has said to her will be accomplished!"

Luke 1:44–45

What a miracle it seems, though it is a daily occurrence in the earth, for new life to be generated within a human body! The child is guarded, nourished within the soft, warm walls of the mother's womb until the moment of readiness. Both mother and child seem united in the desire to come forth. The mother prepares and yearns for this moment, though she knows there will be excruciating pain.

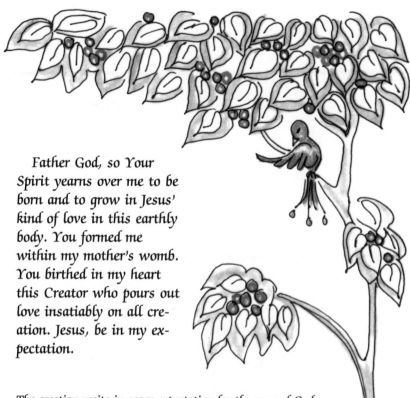

Father God, so Your
Spirit yearns over me to be
born and to grow in Jesus'
kind of love in this earthly
body. You formed me
within my mother's womb.
You birthed in my heart
this Creator who pours out
love insatiably on all creation. Jesus, be in my expectation.

The creation waits in eager expectation for the sons of God
to be revealed. . . . [For] the creation itself will be liberated
from its bondage to decay and brought into the glorious
freedom of the children of God. We know that the whole
creation has been groaning as in the pains of childbirth
right up to the present time.

Romans 8:19, 21–22

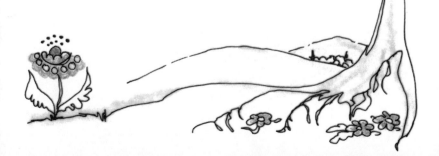

Jesus, Be in My Waiting

*. . . They that wait upon the Lord shall renew their strength;
they shall mount up with wings as eagles; they shall run, and
not be weary; and they shall walk, and not faint.*
Isaiah 40:31, KJV

The writer of Hebrews testified that we are surrounded
by an invisible throng of witnesses. They waited with
confident hope, inspired trust, unquenchable conviction.
Times of waiting are crucial because they demand
endurance and unwavering discipline not to turn
aside onto more pleasant, active paths. Waiting can
be boring, or it can be deliberately infused with
expectant listening for God's way, God's plan
revealed step by step.
Father God, hold me close during the waiting times.
Keep me on the path of Your choosing. Show me what

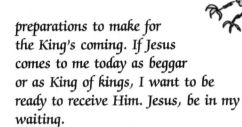

preparations to make for
the King's coming. If Jesus
comes to me today as beggar
or as King of kings, I want to be
ready to receive Him. Jesus, be in my
waiting.

But by faith we eagerly await through the Spirit the
righteousness for which we hope.

Galatians 5:5

Jesus, Be in My Knocking

. . . There was no room for them in the inn.
Luke 2:7

When Mary and Joseph arrived in
Bethlehem, they knocked on every
door seeking a place to rest from
their long journey. I imagine they
wanted a secure, clean, comfortable
room where the baby could be born.
There was no door open to them, no
sterile hospital room, no AAA motel,
no room at all. Jesus was born a
refugee within His own country,
homeless, helpless.
Thirty-three years later Jesus still
had no home. In that last week,
chained, condemned to death,
it seemed that all doors had
closed to the Carpenter,
the maker of doors.

"I am the door," Jesus had said. "I am the gate through which My sheep can go in to rest and out to find pasture." He is still holding that door open for me, but I must open the door of my heart to Him, also. He is knocking. He wants to come in, to rest, to talk over a quiet meal, to explain the Scriptures, to answer my questions. He wants to roll up His sleeves and help me clean out the closets and drawers. He wants to be at home in me, be recognized for who He is in the innermost parts of my being.

Father God, I open the doors of my heart wide to all You have planned for me. Thank You for Jesus' humility and love, which made room for me. Jesus, be in my knocking.

Blessed are those who dwell in your house; they are ever praising you.

Psalm 84:4

Jesus, Be in My Opening

"Ask and it will be given to you; seek and you will find; knock and the door will be opened to you. For everyone who asks receives; he who seeks finds; and to him who knocks, the door will be opened."
Matthew 7:7–8

The innkeeper had had a busy day! It was late. He was worn out from serving so many travelers who had come to Bethlehem for the census. He had made sure each room was clean and ready. Now every available space had been taken.

Who was waking him out of a well-deserved sleep at this hour? From the light of his lantern he could make out the dark, shrouded figures of a bearded man, Galilean from his rustic speech, and a young woman clutching her bulging abdomen, gasping with birth pangs.

This was an emergency.
Well, at least they could lay
her down in the hay. The cave
that sheltered the animals was
cold and dirty, but better than
open ground. Here, use the
lantern. There is water in
the bucket, cold, but better
than nothing.

So the innkeeper made room,
and so I sometimes open my door
to needs around me in just such a
grudging, hesitant way. Jesus often
comes at the unexpected hour
when my life is crowded with
other things.

Father God, I want to open the
doors wide to Jesus whenever He
comes, in whatever form. Flame
in my heart Your welcoming,
generous spirit in spite of how
I feel. Jesus, be in my opening.

Blessed are all who
wait for him!
        Isaiah 30:18

Jesus, Be in My Hospitality

*Do not forget to entertain strangers, for by so doing some people
have entertained angels without knowing it.*
Hebrews 13:2

Though the inn was full and no other rooms in Bethlehem were available, the innkeeper offered Mary and
Joseph use of the stable, probably a cave where horses,
cows and other farm animals stayed. If he had known
who were the guests that starry night, the innkeeper
would have eagerly offered his own bed, the best he
had.

How amazing that the King of the universe was
willing to be born of a humble Jewish girl in a rough
stable, a manger for a bed.

My imagination paints the scene romantically, but I
must not forget the cold, the heavy smells, scratches
from coarse hay, the pain of labor and birth
under unsanitary conditions.

Even though Jesus had no home as
He traveled the hills and valleys of
Israel, He had a way of welcoming
those who came to Him for healing,
deliverance, food, direction,
words of life. The poorest,

those with the most horrible diseases were received tenderly. This is the reign of God on earth.

Father God, show me Your way of hospitality, welcoming those different from myself. Only Your love streaming through me can do this. Jesus, be in my hospitality.

Above all, love each other deeply, because love covers over a multitude of sins. Offer hospitality to one another without grumbling.

1 Peter 4:8–9

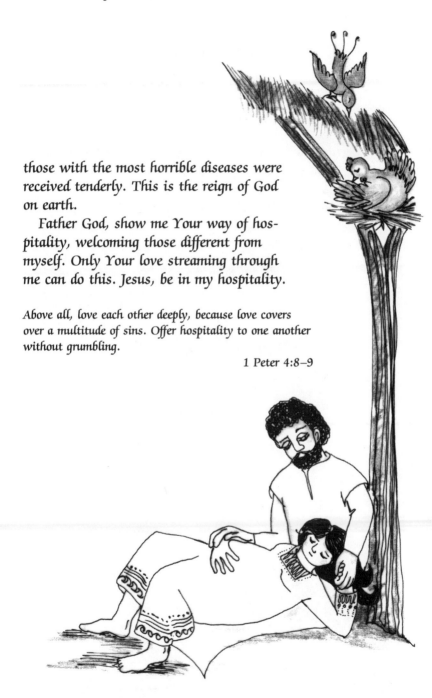

Jesus, Be in My Entering

"When you enter a house, first say, 'Peace to this house.' If a man of peace is there, your peace will rest on him; if not, it will return to you."
Luke 10:5–6

Jesus in me and me in Jesus. Mary experienced this. God entered her, enabling her to begin the pilgrimage that enters into God's Kingdom.

Jesus explained the secret of entering: The gate is narrow; the gate is Jesus Himself, His body broken and His blood poured out for others. I must enter as a child, copying Jesus' obedience, loving God, neighbor and self in God's way and timing. In order to enter, I must rest from my own work. As Jesus enters me, He says *peace* to my heart—to all my struggles to understand, to do what is right, to belong. As I come to others with this gift of aliveness, I say to them, "Peace. Because I have received I can give."

Father God, because Your work is complete in Jesus, I can enter into His rest, which is so much more effective than all my striving. Because I have received of Your inexhaustible riches, I can freely give. Peace to my house this Christmas. Peace to the houses I enter today and the lives I touch. Jesus, be in my entering.

. . . Since we have confidence to enter the Most Holy Place by the blood of Jesus, . . . let us consider how we may spur one another on toward love and good deeds.

Hebrews 10:19, 24

Jesus, Be in My Birthing

. . . The time came for the baby to be born,
and she gave birth to her firstborn, a son.
Luke 2:6–7

The angels rejoiced when Jesus was
born, fulfilling God's plan that had
been foretold hundreds of years before
by many Hebrew prophets. Rome's
Caesar thought he alone ruled over
all the known world, directing the
census from his throne. But even the
detail of the Messiah's birth in Bethlehem had been carefully arranged;
Micah predicted the event.
My physical birth was no accident.
The amazing fragility and complexity
of relationships leading to marriage
and childbirth is cause enough for
wonder. That perfect/imperfect union
that produced me does not compare
with the series of circumstances and
relationships that enables me to be
thoroughly convinced of God's love
for me in Jesus. Both marriage and

birth can describe the tender newness of this "born again" experience. So the angels rejoice!

Father God, through time and space You have called me into the here and now to be Yours, for Jesus to be born in me. Show me Your way to reach out with the good news that You are for everyone. Jesus, be in my birthing.

"Flesh gives birth to flesh, but the Spirit gives birth to spirit. You should not be surprised at my saying, 'You must be born again.' "
                                        John 3:6–7

Jesus, Be in My Groaning

*We know that the whole creation has been
groaning as in the pains of childbirth right
up to the present time. . . . We . . . groan
inwardly as we wait eagerly for our adoption
as sons, the redemption of our bodies.*
Romans 8:22–23

Childbirth is not easy. As the birth
pangs come closer together, the
woman moans, groans, cries out in
the effort. Then comes an incredible
peace, deeper because of the
contrasting struggle.
When Jesus said we must be born
again, of spirit as well as of flesh,
Nicodemus struggled to understand.
Paul knew well that struggle. When
Jesus made Paul blind, he began to
see that the whole universe is like a
woman in labor.
Every part of creation is in a rhythm
of groaning and ecstasy for me, and
for every child of earth, to come forth
new in the perfect likeness of God's
love. Birth is a process that does not

happen all at once, and my spirit groans at times in union with God's Spirit for this holiness to be generated. God's Spirit reveals what is not yet like God; He searches my heart. The Holy Spirit knows me better than I know myself, yet He is for me, interceding, yearning, helping, comforting, guiding like a midwife, until all God's children shine with His likeness.

Father God, You have thought of everything. You have prepared for this birth and even participate actively in the bringing forth. Help me do my part. Jesus, be in my groaning.

"Flesh gives birth to flesh, but the Spirit gives birth to spirit."

John 3:6

Jesus, Be in My Receiving

"I am the Lord's servant," Mary answered. "May it be to me as you have said." Then the angel left her.
Luke 1:38

Both Mary and Joseph received the startling message from angels that God's Spirit would enter history through them, in a specific time, place, race, culture. They were both willing to receive into themselves God's will and its consequences.

Jesus instructed the disciples to wait in Jerusalem after His ascension for the Holy Spirit to be released through them. As when a person recognizes that he/she is in love, Jesus indicated that His followers would recognize and receive His Holy Spirit of love. As the believers walked in harmonious love, forgiving themselves and each other for all the failures of the past, they pleased God. They found they

received tremendous an-
swers to specific prayers
for specific concerns that
God placed on their hearts.

Father God, as I prepare for
Your love to be born anew in
the depths of my being, enable
me to receive all You have. Widen my channel so Your
rivers of living water have room to flow through me
like the great Falls of Niagara! Jesus, be in my receiving.

"But you will receive power when the Holy Spirit comes on you;
and you will be my witnesses in Jerusalem, and in all Judea and
Samaria, and to the ends of the earth."

Acts 1:8

Jesus, Be in My Happiness

*And Mary said, "My soul praises the Lord and my spirit
rejoices in God my Savior. . . ."*
Luke 1:46–47

Immanuel—God with us—is the root meaning of real
happiness. In the Old Testament, the wicked were
"happy" in their luxury and power to get their own.
Happy in that context meant "prosperous" and
"getting ahead." *Happiness* also implied being
honest and being blessed.
David sang that those who love God
are happy because of who He is: Father
to the fatherless, defender of widows,
the One who brings the lonely into
families and leads out the
imprisoned with
singing (Psalm 68).
Yes! Jesus is Immanuel,
God with us!
O happy day!

Father God, let Immanuel be born in me
anew this season so that the song of our
happy love is heard in even the coldest
heart. Jesus, be in my happiness.

"If I then, your Lord and Master, have washed
your feet, ye also ought to wash one another's
feet. For I have given you an example, that ye
should do as I have done to you. . . . If ye
know these things, happy are ye if ye do
them."

John 13:14–15, 17, KJV

Jesus, Be in My Chaos

In the beginning, the Spirit of God moved through the darkness
that covered the deep waters, through the chaos, confusion,
emptiness, hovering over and shaping the intricate balance of life
on planet earth.
Jesus, the light of God, who would be born of a woman by
the power of the Holy Spirit, spoke all things into being and
holds the universe together by His word (see Genesis 1 and
Colossians 1).

Old Testament history tells how the Holy Spirit's
light entered to lift the heavy oppression of ignorance
and evil so that God's way was revealed to men,
women, children of all nations. The Jewish Scriptures
spoke of Jesus and revealed God's plan.

Father God, as I ponder the history of humanity,
especially the horrors committed in Your name, I humbly ask that Your light flood more brilliantly in the
darkness. Fill me and all human creatures with Your
bright goodness, patient kindness, compassionate
healing, generous service. Jesus, be in my chaos.

In the beginning was the Word, and the Word was with God, and the Word was God. He was with God in the beginning. Through him all things were made; without him nothing was made that has been made. In him was life, and that life was the light of men. The light shines in the darkness, but the darkness has not understood it.

John 1:1–5

Jesus, Be in My Darkness

"The eye is the lamp of the body. If your eyes are good, your whole body will be full of light."
Matthew 6:22

When John the Baptist was born, Zechariah, his father, was given insight that the child would prepare the way for One who would rescue people bound by sin and penetrate the powers of spiritual darkness. That One would be like the rising sun, which brings day out of night.

For many years I sensed darkness within, struggled against it, but felt my subconscious was a great abyss in which lurked an ugliness I could not control. Even after receiving Jesus and yielding myself to Him, I still feared the dark side.

There came a time when I felt drawn to ask that God's Holy Spirit move through all my darkness with the light of Jesus, move through all my years, pain, hidden anger and tears to cleanse and liberate. Jesus' light penetrated my darkness, shone over my deep waters in a healing way. His perfect love penetrated my fear. His cleansing blood set a seal on my subconscious.

Father God, I praise You that the sun does not struggle to shine. Simply by moving in the course You set, burning with the energy You gave it, darkness is lifted, the earth warmed, life imparted and renewed. In this season so cold and dark for many, let me shine with Your light that blesses those it touches. Jesus, be in my darkness.

"No one lights a lamp and puts it in a place where it will be hidden. . . ."

Luke 11:33

Jesus, Be in My Enlightenment

*An angel of the Lord appeared to them, and the glory of the Lord
shone around them, and they were terrified. . . . "Do not be
afraid. I bring you good news of great joy . . . for all the people."*
Luke 2:9–10

When one has been living in a dark
place, light is a shock. It is more comfortable to stay where the darkness
soothes the eyes. But all through history and now at this Advent time, God
is reaching out with messengers of light
into the tragic, terrible darkness that is
the norm, the living death that is all
most have known. With laser directness
God seeks to cut me free from all that
would bind me to the darkness. God
desires this great joy of Jesus for
all people.
Father God, as You speak gently
to me, revealing Yourself, Your
plans, Your ways, the path
before me is enlightened.
I can see the next

step. Though sometimes seeing is terrifying because I can see pitfalls, chasms, ugly motivations, Your light also reveals all that delights, that sparkles and dances in brilliance. Jesus, be in my enlightenment.

I pray . . . that the eyes of your heart may be enlightened in order that you may know the hope to which he has called you, the riches of his glorious inheritance in the saints, and his incomparably great power for us who believe.

Ephesians 1:18–19

Jesus, Be in My Shining

*"You are the light of the world. . . . Let your light
shine before men, that they may see your good deeds
and praise your Father in heaven."*
Matthew 5:14, 16

It was prophesied before His birth that Jesus
would be the light of the world, rescuing those
floundering in darkness. On the Mount of
Transfiguration Jesus glowed with such inten-
sity of the Spirit's light that the disciples had
to cover their eyes. This experience revealed
their own doubt and weakness, but it also
caused them to desire even more to reflect
God's glory as Jesus did. They continued to
follow Jesus: through ignorance into wisdom,
through doubt into faith, through persecution
into freeing love. Their faces shone, too. And
just as the disciples were transformed, the
promise is that I am being changed into His
likeness as well.

Father God, as I decide daily
to follow Jesus' shining example,
I deliberately set aside

complaints and arguments in order to have room for the Spirit's fire. I take off the filthy rags of my own way of doing things, my pride and prejudices so that I can be dressed magnificently in armor of light. I want folks around me to notice a difference. Jesus, be in my shining.

Now the Lord is the Spirit. . . . And we, who with unveiled faces all reflect the Lord's glory, are being transformed into his likeness. . . .

2 Corinthians 3:17–18

Jesus, Be in My Caring

*And there were shepherds living out in the
fields nearby, keeping watch over their
flocks at night.*
Luke 2:8

On the hills outside Bethlehem were
kept the perfect lambs set aside for sacrifice in the Temple. Through the days
their shepherds led them to the best
pasture. Through starry or stormy
nights the shepherds guarded them from
harm. While going about these ordinary
tasks an angel startled these humble
Jewish folk with the best news in the
world: The Messiah is born! As if the
heavens could no longer contain their
excitement over this amazing news,
thousands of angels broke through
the tranquil skies with peals of
joyful song.
After going to see for themselves, the
shepherds returned to their work, but
with what a difference! Now their
hearts were alive with the miracle of
what they had seen and heard.
Praise filled them.

Later Jesus told those who would hear, "I am the Good Shepherd." After the resurrection, Jesus called Peter to be a shepherd, too. "Feed My lambs. . . . Take care of My lambs. . . . Feed My sheep."

Father God, Your call on my life is to come adore You. You call me, as a lamb, into a flock where there is leadership, guidance, godly counsel. You call me to shepherd others, too, who can receive nourishment from me. Jesus, be in my caring.

". . . I lay down my life for the sheep."
John 10:15

Jesus, Be in My Watching

"It will be good for those servants whose master finds them watching when he comes. . . ."
Luke 12:37

To watch is to be alert, aware of what is going on around me at all levels, seen and unseen, physical and spiritual. To watch is to be wise, discerning what is good and evil. To watch is to care as the shepherds did, taking turns as they guarded the helpless sheep. In a way all of us are sheep who need to be cared for. But each believer is also given abilities by the Holy Spirit that enable us to care for those entrusted to us. Each Jewish person in the Advent story was watchful, expectant, praying for the Messiah's coming, even as they went about their daily tasks. We must continue to watch and pray because no one knows when He will come back.

Father God, Jesus, the Messiah, has come, and has promised to come again. I want to be ready at whatever hour, in the midst of whatever task. Put on me the bright linen wedding garment of His faith and love. Fill me with His Spirit of praise, prayer and service. Jesus, be in my watching.

The end of all things is near. Therefore be clear minded and self-controlled so that you can pray. Above all, love each other deeply, because love covers over a multitude of sins.

1 Peter 4:7–8

Jesus, Be in My Seeking

"Glory to God in the highest, and on earth peace to men on whom his favor rests." When the angels had left them and gone into heaven, the shepherds said to one another, "Let's go to Bethlehem and see this thing that has happened. . . ."
Luke 2:14–15

The shepherds were watching through the night; it was their job. But that crisp, chill night God broke into their orderly universe with a riot of angels. "What I am doing is more than you have realized," God seemed to be saying. "You are on the right track following My laws, but My Kingdom is more than your rules and regulations. I am alive, present in the tough circumstances of your lives to bring you joy and peace. Seek Me where I am to be found."

The shepherds obeyed these amazing
instructions and found God's
Kingdom on earth in the form
of a newborn peasant Child, His
bed the animals' hay . . . and
they worshiped.

Father God, I want to be
where Your Kingdom is breaking
forth today. Help me recognize
Your glory in the lowly, commonplace
people and events around me.
Replace my anxieties and fears
with the courageous seeking
of Your justice, Your rule on earth.
Jesus, be in my seeking.

"... Seek first his kingdom and his
righteousness, and all these things
will be given to you as well. Therefore
do not worry about tomorrow...."
                    Matthew 6:33–34

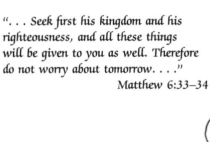

Jesus, Be in My Telling

There is a time for telling and a time for treasuring. The shepherds told everything they had seen and heard, laughing, shouting in the streets, waking up their families and neighbors to tell the good news of the newborn King. As they went back to their work on the hillside, their praises to God kept bubbling over. Theirs was a time of telling.

But for Mary it was a time of treasuring. Too many things had happened that night and from the beginning, nine months before, when the Holy Spirit came into her in a way never known before or since. How could it be? She could share some with Elizabeth, her cousin, whose womb was miraculously opened after being barren so long. Those who suspected her of indiscretion could never understand; no one could, really, because what had happened was an act of God so personal that it defied understanding. No, she could only keep these things in her heart like an immense treasure of which she alone was the caretaker. Maybe the time would come when she could share all with someone, Joseph certainly. Maybe when all had been fulfilled that the angel said, she could share. . . .

Father God, You have given me rich experiences, wonderful evidence of Your work in the world today. Give me the shepherds' overflowing, joyous abandon in sharing and give me Mary's wisdom in knowing when to share. Jesus, be in my telling.

We proclaim to you what we have seen and heard, so that you also may have fellowship with us. And our fellowship is with the Father and with his Son, Jesus Christ.

1 John 1:3

Jesus, Be in My Heart

*But Mary treasured up all these things and pondered
them in her heart.*
Luke 2:19

The heart is the seat of the emotions. Though I
cannot always know what is in my own heart,
what comes from my mouth reveals the anger,
resentment, unhealed wounds that I have
stored there. Unconditional forgiveness of others and God's specific words to me cleanse my
heart. I need to nourish the soil, to weed and
prune in order for the fragrant loveliness of
God's presence to come forth from my heart
naturally. Loving God, neighbors, family
and enemies affects my heart deeply so that
songs of praise well up, blessing me and
others.

Mary stored in her heart those special direc-
tions God gave for her and her family. She did
not understand all the angel said, but as she
praised God, more understanding came. When
Jesus was born and shepherds came to worship,
Mary stored these marvels in her heart as

well. The prophet Simeon told her that a sword would pierce her heart when all took place that God had planned for the Child. As Jesus grew more certain of God's plan for Him and necessarily cut free of the cords binding His heart to Mary's, she continued to ponder, to treasure.

Father God, thank You for Mary's willingness to do Your will even though it meant she would be hurt. Thank You that she was at the cross, at the empty tomb and in the Upper Room at Pentecost. Jesus, be in my heart.

"Love the Lord your God with all your heart. . . ."

Mark 12:30

Jesus, Be in My Loving

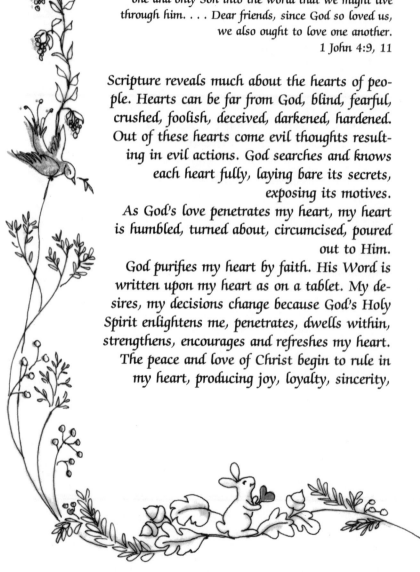

This is how God showed his love among us: He sent his one and only Son into the world that we might live through him. . . . Dear friends, since God so loved us, we also ought to love one another.
1 John 4:9, 11

Scripture reveals much about the hearts of people. Hearts can be far from God, blind, fearful, crushed, foolish, deceived, darkened, hardened. Out of these hearts come evil thoughts resulting in evil actions. God searches and knows each heart fully, laying bare its secrets, exposing its motives.

As God's love penetrates my heart, my heart is humbled, turned about, circumcised, poured out to Him.

God purifies my heart by faith. His Word is written upon my heart as on a tablet. My desires, my decisions change because God's Holy Spirit enlightens me, penetrates, dwells within, strengthens, encourages and refreshes my heart.

The peace and love of Christ begin to rule in my heart, producing joy, loyalty, sincerity, understanding. Even when God tests my heart, it continues to love deeply, make music and make room for others.

Father God, cleanse and create in me a new heart so that I can be a person after Your heart. Jesus, be in my loving.

"To love your neighbor as yourself is more important than all burnt offerings and sacrifices."

Mark 12:33

Jesus, Be in My Temple

When the time of their purification according to the Law of Moses had been completed, Joseph and Mary took [Jesus] to Jerusalem to present him to the Lord.
Luke 2:22

In every aspect of their daily lives, the family of Jesus followed the accepted traditions of the Jewish people in honoring their God. Jesus was/is their expected Messiah, God's Sent One, and it was within their Law that the Baby's unique purpose was recognized. Later, because Jesus' interpretations of the Law conflicted with the people's traditions, Jesus was rejected.

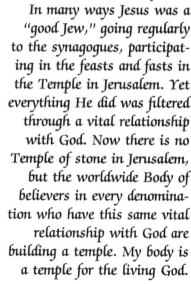

In many ways Jesus was a "good Jew," going regularly to the synagogues, participating in the feasts and fasts in the Temple in Jerusalem. Yet everything He did was filtered through a vital relationship with God. Now there is no Temple of stone in Jerusalem, but the worldwide Body of believers in every denomination who have this same vital relationship with God are building a temple. My body is a temple for the living God.

Come, Holy Spirit, and cleanse this temple—my body, mind and spirit. Fill me with Your holy desires and thoughts, inspire my actions and words. Eliminate every false way so that only what delights You remains in my practice of traditions, in my worship. Jesus, be in my temple.

There is a river whose streams make glad the city of God, the holy place where the Most High dwells.

Psalm 46:4

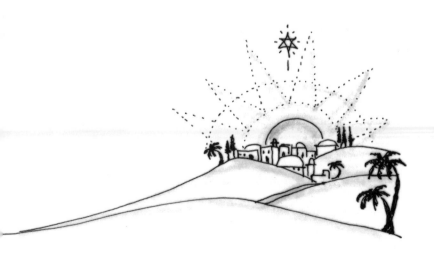

Jesus, Be in My Obedience

. . . "If anyone loves me, he will obey my teaching. My Father will love him, and we will come to him and make our home with him."
John 14:23

Mary and Joseph were each obedient to the *rhema*, the living personal word of God for their lives, obedient to the requirement of their nation's rulers and to the Jewish religious tradition. All these fit together to form God's plan. When the evil plans of King Herod threatened to murder the baby Jesus, Mary and Joseph prayerfully followed God's warning to flee.

Obedience is better than sacrifice. Obedience acts without seeing, is learned by suffering, comes from hearing God's Word and from love.

God's Word teaches me to obey steadfastly, cheerfully. This is the way into life close to God. Obedience makes God's love and joy complete in me and yields eternal salvation

and righteousness. When I obey God,
Satan will war against me, I will be
hated by the world and persecuted. But
if I obey my body with its evil desires,
I will be slave to Satan. The choice
is mine.

Father God, as Jesus learned obedience
through suffering, teach me, too. Today
show me how to honor my parents, and give
respect to my teachers, both physical and
spiritual. Jesus, be in my obedience.

"Surely the righteous still are rewarded; surely there
is a God who judges the earth."

Psalm 58:11

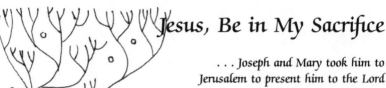

Jesus, Be in My Sacrifice

*. . . Joseph and Mary took him to
Jerusalem to present him to the Lord
. . . and to offer a sacrifice. . . .*
Luke 2:22, 24

The sacrifice God calls me to make
is not doves or lambs, but my own
body, mind and spirit daily brought
to the burning altar of His presence.
Everything not of or like God is to be
burned away. Daily I yield my will
for God's will, my love for His love,
my ambition for His mission. Now
there is no longer a Temple in Jerusalem to which believers may stream
for purification; instead there are
many Christian doctrines, each
claiming the truth and
often denying the others.
None has all the truth, but all
have some truth. My part is to
join with others of like mind as
much as possible, to be led by

God's Spirit in worship and service, to forgive the blindness of others, as I want my own blindness to be healed. A broken and contrite heart God does not despise.

Merciful Father God, I desire to worship You in Spirit and in truth, to receive the cleansing that enables me to be Your healing person in an impure world. Enable me to be built of sturdy stuff, a builder in a broken world. Jesus, be in my sacrifice.

. . . Offer your bodies as living sacrifices, holy and pleasing to God—which is your spiritual worship. Do not conform any longer to the pattern of this world, but be transformed by the renewing of your mind.

Romans 12:1–2

Jesus, Be in My Purifying

Create in me a pure heart, O God, and renew
a steadfast spirit within me.
Psalm 51:10

The Jewish culture and religious tradition encompassed
all the cycles of life and death of God's people. Their
laws stressed the importance of cleanliness, the earliest
health education. After childbirth the mother was
unclean until she had fulfilled certain washings and
come to the Temple with a sacrifice of doves. Mary
fulfilled these laws.
Later Jesus confronted proud religious leaders who
obeyed such rituals of cleansing zealously but had
impure motives.
The common people felt totally unworthy and cut off
from God. Jesus ate with unwashed hands to demon-
strate His identity with those excluded ones. He
taught that purity is not external but a matter of the
heart. In order to be clean before a holy God, the first
step is to recognize that God is the One
who cleanses. All my good works and

intentions are as filthy rags. My part is to accept the Holy Spirit's conviction of sin, reject Satan's false accusations, and bring all I am, the good, bad and ugly, to Jesus.

The blood of Jesus cleanses. The words of Jesus prune. The name of Jesus justifies. Signs of a pure life are singlemindedness, obedience resulting in sincere love, and overcoming.

Create in me a clean heart, O God, and renew a right spirit within me. Jesus, be in my purifying.

Yes, Lord, walking in the way of your laws, we wait for you; your name and renown are the desire of our hearts.

                           Isaiah 26:8

Jesus, Be in My Purpose

"... Because of the tender mercy of our God, by
which the rising sun will come to us from heaven
to shine on those living in darkness ... to
guide our feet into the path of peace."
Luke 1:78–79

The promise of God was fulfilled in Jesus. He
grew from a tiny baby, day by day learning God's
voice in order to understand His part in the grand
plan of the universe.
God formed me in my mother's womb and called
me from my father's house to fulfill my part as
well. I am part of the promise and the promises
enable me to fulfill God's purpose for my life.
Jesus' purpose was to reveal God's love-nature,
which reaches out with forgiveness. This is my purpose as well. As this joy dawns on me, in me, more
and more I will be living in the promise and purpose
for which I was made.

Father God, with the rising of Your
Son each day in my heart, renew Your
covenant promise and reveal Your holy
purpose. I want to walk with You wherever You go, whether it is in fragrant
gardens or through the trash heaps of
this world. Jesus, be in my purpose.

"But for you who revere my name,
the sun of righteousness will rise
with healing in its wings. . . ."
Malachi 4:2

Jesus, Be in My Plans

May he give you the desire of your heart and
make all your plans succeed.
Psalm 20:4

Mary and Joseph planned their en-
gagement, but God had other plans.
Mary and Joseph planned to dedicate
their baby and then take Him back
to Nazareth by the normal route,
but God had other plans. King Herod
tried to kill the Child who was a
threat to his power, but God had
other plans.
God has a perfect plan for every one
in His creation. Only God knows all
the circumstances and relationships
that touch and shape me and the
flow of history.
In spite of all the pressures of the
world to conform to its ways, in
spite of my own weaknesses and sinful nature, in spite of the hate-filled
strategies of Satan's furious forces, I
can seek and find God's path.
God is committed to me.

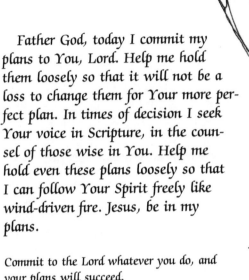

Father God, today I commit my plans to You, Lord. Help me hold them loosely so that it will not be a loss to change them for Your more perfect plan. In times of decision I seek Your voice in Scripture, in the counsel of those wise in You. Help me hold even these plans loosely so that I can follow Your Spirit freely like wind-driven fire. Jesus, be in my plans.

Commit to the Lord whatever you do, and your plans will succeed.

Proverbs 16:3

Jesus, Be in My Spirit

For you did not receive a spirit that makes you a slave again to fear, but you received the Spirit of sonship. And by him we cry, "Abba, Father." The Spirit himself testifies with our spirit that we are God's children.
Romans 8:15–16

To the Temple Mary and Joseph brought two doves, the sacrifice required for a firstborn son. At Jesus' baptism a dove appeared from heaven; it was the Holy Spirit. "You are My Son, whom I love," said the Father. "With You I am well pleased."

As I offer the best I have to what I know of God, He blesses me with His best, the Holy Spirit. And that Holy Spirit, who hovered over the chaos in the beginning and brought order, light, beauty and life, now moves on the waters of my life to create something new.

Father God, my spirit, like a dove, likes to soar freely, but needs to be yielded as a living sacrifice to You. Within Your love are many opportunities to glide on glistening wings of prayer, but help me hear and obey when You call me to give up that freedom in exchange for costly service. Unite my spirit with Your Spirit so that I can discern Your timing for transferring pure praise into humble ministry. Jesus, be in my spirit.

[Your beauty] should be that of your inner self, the unfading beauty of a gentle and quiet spirit, which is of great worth in God's sight.

1 Peter 3:4

Jesus, Be in My Rejoicing

Dear friends, do not be surprised at the painful trial you are suf-
fering. . . . But rejoice that you participate in the sufferings of
Christ, so that you may be overjoyed when his glory is revealed.
1 Peter 4:12–13

The Scriptures are filled with rejoicing as a result of
the good news of God's love for us in Jesus. The heavens and earth rejoice. Little hills, fields, mountains,
trees, as well as the saints, the seekers of the living
God, rejoice. I rejoice with my heart, soul, spirit,
tongue, lips. The virgin rejoices in the dance. The be-
reaved rejoice from the depths of their sorrow. Workers
rejoice in the labor of their hands. Elderly rejoice in
years lived. Youth rejoice in their vitality. Parents rejoice when their children know God. A husband
rejoices in the wife of his youth. Sower and reaper
rejoice together. Those persecuted for their faith rejoice
in being counted worthy to suffer.

Believers in Jesus rejoice in hope of glory, in God's mercy, salvation, God's Word and promises, in the Truth, in our names written in the Book of Life. We rejoice when one part is honored. We rejoice with the angels when one lost lamb is found.

Father God, thank You for this season of rejoicing. Thank You for Your joy unspeakable and full of glory. Jesus, be in my rejoicing.

. . . Even though you do not see him now, you believe in him and are filled with an inexpressible and glorious joy.

1 Peter 1:8

Jesus, Be in My Thanking

I thank my God every time I remember you. In all my prayers for all of you, I always pray with joy because of your partnership . . . being confident of this, that he who began a good work in you will carry it on to completion until the day of Christ Jesus.
Philippians 1:3–6

Anna gave thanks to God when she saw the baby Jesus at His dedication in the Temple; she sensed that this child was special. Later Jesus demonstrated that all life is holy, every meal a time to offer thanks to God.
In spite of beatings, imprisonments, shipwrecks and more, Paul, in almost every letter, urged everyone to be thankful to God and thankful for each other.
Paul thanked God for their faithfulness, growth, strength, love, ministry, generosity, perseverance in persecutions. He urged us to give thanks in prayer with intercession, with our lips, for our daily food, at all times and in everything. He thanked God continually for leading the believers in victory, for the indescribable gift of Jesus, most of all for God Himself.

Father God, Your infinite goodness and love are worthy of an eternity of thanksgiving. Jesus, be in my thanking.

Thanks be to God, who always leads us in triumphal procession in Christ and through us spreads everywhere the fragrance of the knowledge of him.
2 Corinthians 2:14

Jesus, Be in My Looking Forward

But you, dear friends, build yourselves up in your most holy faith and pray in the Holy Spirit. Keep yourselves in God's love as you wait for the mercy of our Lord Jesus Christ to bring you to eternal life. Be merciful to those who doubt. . . .

Jude 20–22

Old Anna, widow for most of her eighty years, had a lot to complain about. She had a right to feel sorry for herself. Instead Anna chose to look forward to the coming of the Messiah. Thus she recognized Him even when He came disguised as a child of poverty.

If I am bound by sinful habits and do not have the will to be free of them, looking forward is cause for apprehension, fear of judgment, even terror. If I put my sinful self in Jesus' hands, the future means expecting His coming to complete what He has begun in me, purifying me from wickedness that perhaps I don't even realize.

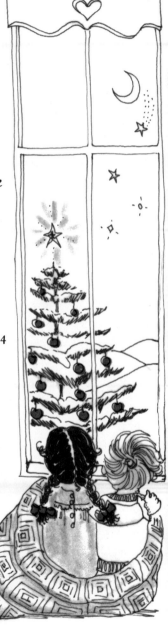

Father God, Christmas is a time of
looking forward with expectation to
Jesus' coming—to His being born in me
anew, growing, teaching, performing
miracles, dying, rising again, empower-
ing. Come quickly, Lord Jesus. Jesus,
be in my looking forward.

To him who is able to keep you from falling
and to present you before his glorious presence
without fault and with great joy. . . .

Jude 24

Jesus, Be in My Perseverance

Now there was a man in Jerusalem called Simeon, who was righteous and devout. He was waiting for the consolation of Israel, and the Holy Spirit was upon him. It had been revealed to him by the Holy Spirit that he would not die before he had seen the Lord's Christ.

Luke 2:25–26

Simeon was old but he had not given up hope. The promise was alive in him that he would not die until he had seen the Messiah. So his waiting was expectant. His relating with others was alert—maybe this was the one. He had to be ready at any moment to hear the call, recognize God's chosen One from among the crowds.

Now the Messiah Jesus has come. Now my call is to help bring His Kingdom to earth as it is in heaven. I must go through counter-influences, opposition or discouragement in order to enter into God's promises. Through all the testings and trials, I learn who God is, that He is trustworthy. I learn that in God is the answer

and resource to meet every
need in His way and timing.

Father God, reveal to me the
selfishness of my prayers.
Show me how the difficulties I
face today fit into Your plan.
Show me how to overcome.
Jesus, be in my perseverance.

"But the seed on good soil stands for
those with a noble and good heart,
who hear the word, retain it, and by
persevering produce a crop."

Luke 8:15

Jesus, Be in My Abounding

". . . My eyes have seen your salvation, which you have prepared in the sight of all people, a light for revelation to the Gentiles and for glory to your people Israel."
Luke 2:30–32

The moment that for Simeon was the culmination of a life dedicated to God was for Jesus and His family just the beginning. God had given Simeon and Anna a certain role to play—to wait, to intercede, to watch for the Messiah's coming. They knew their part and were faithful. They recognized the answer even when it came in unexpected form. Jesus had the lead part in this universal drama and revealed the heavenly Father's love in fullest form. Even when Jesus' earthly ministry culminated in death and resurrection, that was only a beginning for the believers. These past 2,000 years have been an opportunity for each life touched by the glory of this story to multiply magnificently the "greater things" Jesus promised we would do. Every day is an opportunity to leave behind past

failures, discover my part and continue
faithfully.

Father God, You are the One who
enables me to be faithful. Pour out
on me the abundance of gifts needed
to communicate Your healing presence
in this hurting world. Grow in me the
abundance of fruit needed to nourish
and sustain life in the Spirit. Jesus,
be in my abounding.

. . . Live in him, rooted and built up in him,
strengthened in the faith as you were taught,
and overflowing with thankfulness.
                                    Colossians 2:6–7

Jesus, Be in My Seeing

"... Lord, ... now dismiss your servant in peace. For
my eyes have seen your salvation, which you have prepared in the sight of all people, a light for revelation to
the Gentiles and for glory to your people Israel."
Luke 2:29–32

The birth of Jesus was accompanied by a new
way of seeing, a Holy Spirit-inspired understanding of the meaning of God's acts in history. Zechariah, the elderly father of John the
Baptist, and Mary, Jesus' young mother, both
spoke out prophetic understandings about the
future. God's salvation was the focus for all
who would accept His control, both individuals
and nations. The rich and powerful would
crumble. The poor would be blessed by Jesus'
new world order.

Though I can see and understand only imper-
fectly, as I am filled with God's loving Spirit to
overflowing, I am assured of being fully known
and understood. This same Spirit enables me to
see Satan's deceptions and avoid the pitfalls in

this pilgrim way of bringing God's Kingdom to earth as it is in heaven. He gives me illuminating dreams, prophecies and visions.

Father God, I trust You to reveal to me what I need to understand about the past and show me how I need to prepare for the future. Be in my vision, my dreams. Jesus, be in my seeing.

"In the last days, God says, I will pour out my Spirit on all people. Your sons and daughters will prophesy. . . ."

Acts 2:17

Jesus, Be in My Beholding

And we, who with unveiled faces all reflect the Lord's glory, are being transformed into his likeness with ever-increasing glory, which comes from the Lord, who is the Spirit.
2 Corinthians 3:18

Simeon praised God that his eyes beheld the baby Jesus. Though his natural eyes may have been dimmed by years and tears, his spiritual sight was sharp, quickened by holding this particular baby at this particular time.
Jesus repeatedly demonstrated this same kind of intuitive discernment, this inner knowing that sees to the heart. This beholding is a gift Jesus gives me in the Holy Spirit as I walk more by faith and less by questioning doubts and fears. This seeing also means being in vibrant contact with the living God so that I become a reflection of His glory.

Father God, in these critical, desperate times
for our planet, I need to see and reflect Your
glory. I need to know what You are doing to create a new heaven and earth, and what my part is.
Wash me of all that dims my spiritual eyes.
Jesus, be in my beholding.

Jesus looked at him and loved him. "One thing you lack,"
he said. "Go, sell everything you have and give to the poor,
and you will have treasure in heaven. Then come, follow
me."

Mark 10:21

Jesus, Be in My Wounds

Then Simeon blessed them and said to Mary, his mother: "This child is destined to cause the falling and rising of many in Israel, and to be a sign that will be spoken against, so that the thoughts of many hearts will be revealed. And a sword will pierce your own soul too."
Luke 2:34–35

The blessing of God does not mean that everything will be easy and comfortable. After Simeon's blessing, he warned Mary that this Child would change the way things had always been done in Israel, in the world. There would be violent disagreements. Powers would clash, a sword would pierce their souls.

The conflict over who Jesus says He is continues. Every person who hears of Him must decide if He is Lord. And if He is Lord, He is due total allegiance. That rubs against the grain of all other people and institutions that demand my time, resources, allegiance, homage. I will be involved with some of these, but as a representative of God's kind of government, I will be an advocate for the poor, homeless, hungry, blind, imprisoned, sick. Being involved with these people in the name of Jesus will hurt, but it is also where the blessing of His presence abounds.

Father God, help me not to cringe from the wounds You allow. I need Your courage, Your vision, Your determination, Your healing. Jesus, be in my wounds.

"The King will reply, 'I tell you the truth, whatever you did for one of the least of these brothers of mine, you did for me.' "
                              Matthew 25:40

Jesus, Be in My Tests

*If any man builds on this foundation using
gold, silver, costly stones, wood, hay or straw,
his work will be shown for what it is. . . .*
1 Corinthians 3:12–13

Mary was warned that the blessing God
was giving her would be painfully tested.
She would suffer wounds in her own soul.
Her ancestors had learned much about
God's testings. Abraham's promised son
was placed on the altar. Joseph's dreams
were tested through iron shackles on
bruised feet, a rich woman's lust and two
years in prison. Satan tested Job through
robbers, murderers, wind, fire and even
through the nagging of his wife and
misunderstanding of his friends.
If Satan seemed to have his way for a
time, it was because God allowed it. The
assurance is that God is always vic-
torious and enables us to endure, even
gain patience, hope and joy through the
refining process.

Mary must have remembered the prophetic words about a sword piercing her soul as she wept at the foot of the cross. Perhaps later she touched the sword's wound, as did Thomas, in wonder at the vindication of all her son had said and done.

Father God, help me to count as blessing the trials and tests that purify and shape me into Your useful vessel. Jesus, be in my tests.

For our light and momentary troubles are achieving for us an eternal glory that far outweighs them all.

2 Corinthians 4:17

Jesus, Be in My Rulers

*After Jesus was born in Bethlehem in Judea, during the time of
King Herod, Magi from the east came to Jerusalem and asked,
"Where is the one who has been born king of the Jews?" . . .
"Out of you [Bethlehem] will come a ruler who will be the
shepherd of my people Israel."*
Matthew 2:1–2, 6

Each of the rulers in the first Christmas story knew
that his powers were limited. The Magi sought to
worship the baby born as King, representative of the
highest power, God. King Herod was the opposite; he
was a grasping, fawning dictator. Superstitious and
half-believing in the Jewish God, Herod yearned after
personal power and wealth. He even had his own sons
killed in jealous fear for his throne.

In whatever country I am, under whatever kind of
rulers, my responsibility is to pray for those in
power—requests, prayers, intercession
and thanksgiving. No government
is perfect; each one needs citizens
filled with the dynamite power
of God's Holy Spirit to
overcome injustice. Those in
countries with rulers who, like

Herod, oppress and torture their own people especially need prayer and the good news that the baby King born under just such circumstances is now King over all kings.

Father God, show me how to relate to those who rule. Give me wisdom in my requests, prayers, intercession and work for positive change. Open my eyes to see genuine reasons to give thanks. Jesus, be in my rulers.

. . . Requests, prayers, intercession and thanksgiving [should] be made for everyone—for kings and all those in authority, that we may live peaceful and quiet lives in all godliness and holiness.

1 Timothy 2:1–2

Jesus, Be in My Authorities

Everyone must submit himself to the governing authorities, for there is no authority except that which God has established. . . .
Romans 13:1

Jesus submitted to the earthly authorities of family, religion and government. Yet Jesus was willing to suffer the consequences from those authorities when He had to go against them. Jesus went against authorities only when they were counter to God's way and plan. So in tune was He with God's creation that He could speak and winds and waves obeyed. Jesus did not hesitate to come against Satan's authority when being tempted to meet His own needs. God's compassion moved Him to use authority against Satan's binding of others. Jesus freed people from sickness, poverty, demon possession, fear, blindness, paralysis, materialism, even death. To His followers, to me, He gave authority to bind and to loose. Jesus said I should expect to see greater works than He had done as I walk in His steps.

Father God, please give me discernment to see with Your eyes the things You would have me bind and loose in this season. Help me use my authority in ways pleasing to You. Jesus, be in my authority and authorities.

For our struggle is not against flesh and blood, but against the . . . authorities, against the powers of this dark world. . . . Therefore put on the full armor of God. . . .

Ephesians 6:12–13

Jesus, Be in My Searching

[The Magi said,] "We saw his star in the east and have come to worship him." . . . Then Herod called the Magi secretly and found out from them the exact time the star had appeared.
Matthew 2:2, 7

The Bible is a book of searching and finding, of longing and fulfillment. The entire creation yearns in agony for every pitiful human creature to know that God's glorious plan is perfect for him or her. Christmas is God's answer to the longing and searching of every man, woman and child. Jesus' birth, humbly, quietly in me, causes the heavens to ring with joyous song.

Jesus in me is the end of the restless struggles in the core of my being. In Jesus is the answer to all my questions and searchings for truth and meaning, vocation, understanding, wisdom, healing. Not that I know all—immediately or ever—but in being known is the beginning of the end of my search.

Now I know where to look, just as the one
who has a treasure map discovers the
X-marked spot and begins to dig there.

Father God, thank You for seeking me out
before I ever knew You. Thank You for Your
gift of life and for the restlessness I have
when not centered in You. Thank You for
Your perfect plan, which reveals Your love
more and more as I search for You. Jesus, be
in my searching.

*You will find him if you look for him with all your
heart and with all your soul.*

Deuteronomy 4:29

Jesus, Be in My Finding

After they had heard the king, [the Magi] went on their way, and the star they had seen in the east went ahead of them until it stopped over the place where the child was. When they saw the star, they were overjoyed. On coming to the house, they saw the child with his mother Mary. . . .
Matthew 2:9–11

The wise men had been seeking the One born King of the Jews. No one knows from what country they came or what studies led them to leave home seeking. It is clear that God wanted them to find the Baby because He put signs in the heavens and in ancient prophecies that led them, enabling them to find.

God's Word tells me to seek Him with all my heart, soul, mind and strength. I am to seek God in the morning, and continually. He calls me to seek His face while humbly turning from my wicked ways. If I seek God and His Kingdom above all else, the promise is repeated often: God will be found, and He will hear, heal and provide.

Father God, like the wise men I come seeking You, sometimes from far places. You are behind me, before me, underneath me, above me and in me. In You I live and move and have my fullest being. Jesus, be in my finding.

"Seek the Lord while he may be found; call on him while he is near."

Isaiah 55:6

Jesus, Be in My Giving

On coming to the house, they saw the child with his mother Mary, and they bowed down and worshiped him. Then they opened their treasures and presented him with gifts of gold and of incense and of myrrh.
Matthew 2:11

The wise men brought the best they had to the Christ Child. Jesus told Matthew to look for Him in the poor, the foreigner, the sick, the imprisoned, the hungry, the naked. These are usually people who can do very little for themselves. These are people with needs to whom my giving could be significant. So many times Christmas giving degenerates into a frantic search for gifts appropriate for family and friends who already have more than they need. The joy of giving decreases and, instead, abounds the stress of "Oh, I failed to get 'so and so' something, and she gave me this, which costs $———." So the pressures increase and the Christmas spirit, which includes the spirit of giving, slips sorrowfully away.
Father God, it takes courage to break the cycle. Help me this season to put priority on giving to

Jesus through those who really have needs. Awaken the spirit of Christmas joy in me, in my family, in those who have so much and in those who have too little. Help me give in such a way that the receiver can see his/her value as a child of God. Jesus, be in my giving.

Each man should give what he has decided in his heart to give, not reluctantly or under compulsion, for God loves a cheerful giver.
2 Corinthians 9:7

Jesus, Be in My Sharing

*And do not forget to do good and to share with others, for
with such sacrifices God is pleased.*
Hebrews 13:16

God gives to me that I may share with those in
need. God gives me work so that I am not tempted
to take what is not mine and so that I have something to share. Sometimes my heart is hardened by
the many demands. Sometimes I withdraw from seeing the needs of others. When my own desires are at
the center of my attention, I do not want to see
others' needs or share. I feel angry at the needy
person and his condition, frustrated and helpless
at the economic or political situations that
create masses of poverty and injustice.
Yet God's Word does not wince when confronted
with the poor. Governments are judged
and so are those who "have" by their
response to the poor. Sharing in a
way that is personal, loving,
life-building, as if among
family, is the
example Jesus

and His followers showed. Sharing is the Christmas spirit year-'round!

Father God, forgive my greediness as I forgive the greed of others. Forgive my hardness of heart as I forgive the hardness I see in others, for closing my eyes to needs as I forgive those who seem blind. Forgive me for not sharing when I sense Your gentle call to do so. Jesus, be in my sharing.

Now if we are children, then we are heirs—heirs of God and co-heirs with Christ, if indeed we share in his sufferings in order that we may also share in his glory.

Romans 8:17

Jesus, Be in My Giving

The kings of Tarshish and of distant shores will bring tribute to him; the kings of Sheba and Seba will present him gifts. All kings will bow down to him and all nations will serve him.
Psalm 72:10–11

The special gifts brought by the Magi to the Christ Child seem strange until their meanings are explored. Gold, universal symbol of wealth, was given to this tiny King of kings. Frankincense, the fragrant gum resin, was the main ingredient used in the incense burned in the Temple. Frankincense was set before the Holy of Holies with the Bread of the Presence. Myrrh, an important ingredient of the sacred anointing oil in Exodus, was used in perfumes and for burial preparations. Jesus refused the wine mixed with myrrh on the cross.

So the gifts of the wise men had meaning beyond their physical value. They told that Jesus' life would be royal, anointed, holy, close to God, yet one of suffering and death.

As I consider the ones to whom I will give gifts this Christmas, Father God, illumine my thoughts to perceive what gifts speak of Your plan for them. Let my gifts be appropriate for each individual. Open them to the mystery and possibility of what You have ahead. Jesus, be in my giving.

Ascribe to the Lord the glory due his name; bring an offering and come into his courts.

Psalm 96:8

Jesus, Be in My Gifts

"If you, then, though you are evil, know how to give good gifts to your children, how much more will your Father in heaven give good gifts to those who ask him!"
Matthew 7:11

When I remember Christmases past, gifts played such a big part. Growing up after the Depression, we made most of our gifts, beginning early in the fall to plan, gather materials and prepare something special for each family member and friend.

Studying the Sears catalog as a wish book and making a list of what I wanted filled many hours, too. My parents always made Christmas a giving time—of themselves as well as material things.

The warm cinnamony smell from Mama's kitchen, the hum of her sewing machine and the crisp cedar curls in Daddy's workshop spoke of caring.

Still, I remember that my wants were usually greater than what I received. Sometimes I did not like my gifts and had to struggle with polite acceptance. I knew my parents gave the best they could with love.

Father God, thank You for those who have given to me: for my parents, brother and sister, my husband, his parents and extended family. Thank You for those who have given through the years to enable our ministry. Thank You for Your own giving nature, and that best gift of all, Your Son, Jesus. Father, this Christmas help me choose gifts that represent Your kind of love. Jesus, be in my gifts.

Share with God's people who are in need.
Romans 12:13

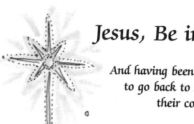

Jesus, Be in My Journey

And having been warned in a dream not to go back to Herod, they returned to their country by another route.
Matthew 2:12

The wise men, too, had a dream that gave them direction, warning them to go home by another way. The Herods of this world are to be avoided because their ambition dirties their motives and destroys those in their way.

Life is a journey, and so is death a part of the whole. The road is of my own choosing, though my starting place has been determined. Life's journey can be filled with light or swallowed by darkness, but the promise is that the Light of the world will neither leave me nor forsake me.

At Christmas many journey to the lighted hearths of their youth, to wherever "home" is now. Some find a deep sadness, a grief that the joy of this season is found only in surface material things. The longing is for true unity, understanding, being heard and hearing, being loved and loving. The gulfs of generations, of values, of music and of what is meaningful often cannot be crossed. The journey the heart makes is not easy, but it cannot settle for less than the bridge of acceptance and unconditional love.

Father God, this Christmas, after finding in Your birth my true "home," let my journey always be in Your steps, in Your joy, in Your peace, even in Your suffering. Jesus, be in my journey.

Jesus returned to Galilee in the power of the Spirit, and news about him spread through the whole countryside.

Luke 4:14

Jesus, Be in My Visiting

*"I needed clothes and you clothed me, I was sick and you looked
after me, I was in prison and you came to visit me."*
Matthew 25:36

The kings left their normal, comfortable routine, jour-
neying far to visit the One born to fulfill God's promise. Christmas is a time of visiting, whether dropping
in on neighbors or following distant stars to family
and friends seldom seen. My visiting takes on new
meaning when considered in the light of the Messiah's
star. As an ambassador of the Kingdom of love, as
royal priest and minister I represent Jesus to those I
visit. As part of God's people, only because of His
mercy and grace can I communicate mercy and
grace.

Jesus said that He would be present when we visit
the sick, the imprisoned, those unwelcome, those in
need. Jesus is present in suffering, and when He is
recognized He makes it redemptive. He is present in
me in gifts of healing touch, listening ears, cheerful
smiles, words of understanding,
encouragement or a song.

Father God, show me who needs me to visit. Urge me from my comfort to reach out with the gifts You have given me. I know the kings received much more than they gave in their visit to the baby King Jesus. Jesus, be in my visiting.

Dear friends, I urge you, as aliens and strangers in the world, to . . . [live] such good lives among the pagans that, though they accuse you of doing wrong, they may see your good deeds and glorify God on the day he visits us.

1 Peter 2:11–12

Jesus, Be in My Danger

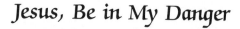

When they had gone, an angel of the Lord appeared to Joseph in a dream. "Get up," he said, "take the child and his mother and escape to Egypt. Stay there until I tell you, for Herod is going to search for the child to kill him." So he got up, took the child and his mother during the night and left for Egypt.
Matthew 2:13–14

God's protection was with Mary, Joseph and Jesus. God's purposes could not be stopped by a cruel king's murderous jealousy. Even the parents of the young boys killed by Herod's fury could be comforted by knowing that God had shown them through prophecies of old that this would happen. God understands our grief and comforts us in it.

Where I can freely choose, my place is always to seek God's perfect will. Where ones controlled by the evil one make my choices for me, God is my refuge, strength, shelter, ever-present help. Like Shadrach, Meshach and Abednego, I can say about the evil king's fiery furnace, ". . . The God we serve is able to save us from it, and he will rescue us from your hand, O king. But even if he does not, we want you to know, O king, that we will not serve your gods or worship the image of gold you have set up" (Daniel 3:17–18).

Father God, reveal to me the dangers around me and my loved ones so that we can take refuge in You. Keep me from the dangers of my own angry words and actions, from the danger of blasphemy against Your Holy Spirit. Jesus, be in my danger.

Let the morning bring me word of your unfailing love, for I have put my trust in you.

Psalm 143:8

Jesus, Be in My Call

So he got up, took the child and his mother during the night and left for Egypt, where he stayed until the death of Herod. And so was fulfilled what the Lord had said through the prophet: "Out of Egypt I called my son."
Matthew 2:14–15

God called the holy family out of Egypt to return to Israel. This positioning was important for the fulfillment of God's plan. Jesus said He did not come to call the righteous but sinners to repentance. He told of the king's wedding feast where friends and poverty-stricken street people were called to come and participate. Paul reminded the believers that not many of them were noble, powerful, well-educated or wealthy when they received God's call.

The call is to conform to the likeness of Jesus, to be justified and glorified. I am God's servant and laborer, but Jesus calls me friend, sister, daughter of God, saint. God's calling includes ministry gifts of the Spirit. I am called out of darkness to light, to cleanness, to eternal life, to peace, into liberty and glory in one hope. All things work together for good to those called according to God's purpose.

Father God, when I am in Your secret place of intimacy and call to You, You will answer, rescue, be with me in trouble. Help me to respond quickly and with all my heart, soul, mind and strength to Your call. Jesus, be in my call.

If I say, "Surely the darkness will hide me. . . ," even the darkness will not be dark to you; the night will shine like the day. . . .

Psalm 139:11–12

Jesus, Be in My Mourning

*When Herod realized that he had been outwitted by the
Magi, he was furious, and he gave orders to kill all the
boys in Bethlehem and its vicinity who were two
years old and under. . . .*
Matthew 2:16

To participate fully in the coming of Jesus, in His
being born into the human condition, is to mourn
with Rachel for her children who were no more.
The result of good coming into the world to re-
deem is that evil lashes out in wild fury. What
was taken for granted as Satan's territory is now
called into question. Good will overcome evil, but
not without a battle. How many mothers have
grieved in the past 2,000 years because of greed,
fear and corrupted use of power by the Herods of
this world? How many mothers grieve right now
this Christmas season?
Paul, who in his own body experienced hate and
rejection because of the Good News, taught that
there are two kinds of grief. There is human grief,
which leads to death because it refuses to be comforted. And there is godly grief, which is anguish,
too, but it "brings repentance

that leads to salvation and leaves no regret"
(2 Corinthians 7:10). Jesus took on the cross
Rachel's griefs and felt her bitter cries and
aching loneliness for the loss of her sons.

Father God, in this joyous Christmas season,
there are people who mourn, people heavily bur-
dened by grief. Open a window of comfort for
them. Enable them to sense Jesus' coming, which
removes the sting of death, the bitterness of grief.
Jesus, be in my mourning.

Comfort, comfort my people, says your God.

                                              Isaiah 40:1

Jesus, Be in My Comfort

After Herod died, an angel of the Lord appeared in a dream to Joseph in Egypt and said, "Get up, take the child and his mother and go to the land of Israel, for those who were trying to take the child's life are dead."
Matthew 2:19–20

The poignancy of those suffering Jewish mothers in Bethlehem at the time when the most glorious and joyous event occurred there strikes me with great force. Still there are conflict and weeping in Bethlehem. Now Christian Arab mothers weep for their children. The cycle of suffering and mourning continues, but so does the hope and reality of comfort. In compassion there is healing. In comfort there is renewed hope that a new beginning is possible.

In intercession God leads me to participate in the suffering of my brothers and sisters everywhere: Catholics and Protestants in Ireland; blacks and whites in Soweto, South

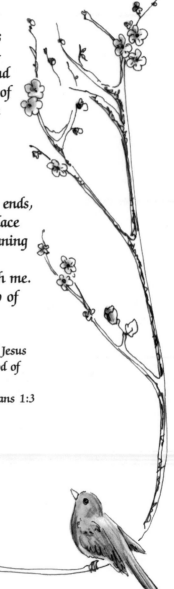

Africa, and my own South; landless
poor and tortured in Central America;
those everywhere who wander, homeless, or live in shacks of cardboard and
plastic. Those who call on the name of
Jesus, who have two of anything, are
elected to participate in the mission
of mercy, of sharing, of putting a
human face on statistics and making
the suffering redemptive.

Father God, as this Advent season ends,
I know a new beginning has taken place
in me because of focusing on the meaning
of Your Son's birth. Show me those
whose lives You would touch through me.
Bring Your blessing out of every drop of
suffering. Jesus, be in my comfort.

Praise be to the God and Father of our Lord Jesus
Christ, the Father of compassion and the God of
all comfort.

2 Corinthians 1:3

Jesus, Be in My Growing

When Joseph and Mary had done everything required by the Law of the Lord, they returned to Galilee to their own town of Nazareth. And the child grew and became strong; he was filled with wisdom, and the grace of God was upon him.
Luke 2:39–40

The entire Bible portrays God's pouring out His favor on individuals, families and peoples. God's favor was given to Abel because of his sacrifice, to Abraham for his intercession, to Moses for leadership, to Samuel for judgment, to the youth David as he stood before King Saul, to Nehemiah, Esther and Daniel before foreign kings. Mary, Jesus' mother, was favored as were the disciples of Jesus after Pentecost.

Favor is like a cloud of latter rain, like dew on the grass, says Proverbs. Favor is acceptance, pleasure, delight; it is gracious, kind, pleasant and precious. Following the example of the Child Jesus who grew in favor with God and man, I am to

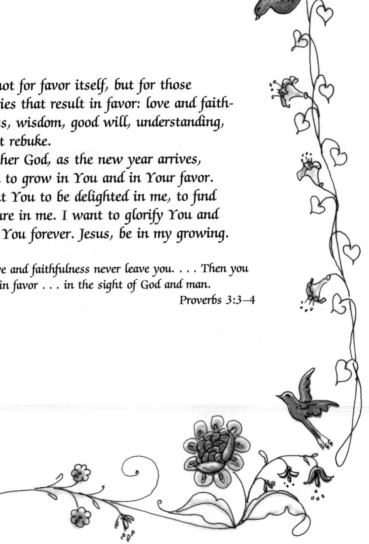

seek not for favor itself, but for those
qualities that result in favor: love and faithfulness, wisdom, good will, understanding,
honest rebuke.

Father God, as the new year arrives,
I seek to grow in You and in Your favor.
I want You to be delighted in me, to find
pleasure in me. I want to glorify You and
enjoy You forever. Jesus, be in my growing.

*Let love and faithfulness never leave you. . . . Then you
will win favor . . . in the sight of God and man.*
Proverbs 3:3–4

Jesus, Be in My Grace

. . . Grow in the grace and knowledge of our
Lord and Savior Jesus Christ.
2 Peter 3:18

Christmas, Jesus' coming into the world
as a baby, is God's generous gift to
me, His grace and truth in tiny human
form. That grace grew and He grew in
grace; then He gave His grace to those
who believe in Him. Grace is gracious-
ness, which reflects in our lives and
includes gratitude, joy, generosity,
thankfulness. Grace is the gift of God's
Holy Spirit given according to His plan,
which is good. When I am humble I
can receive God's grace, which is suffi-
cient, grace to help in time of need. I
am to live by God's grace and not by
my own efforts, striving, accomplish-
ments. The message of grace in the
book of Acts is that there were no
needy people among the believers.
Father God, as the old year slips away
and the new begins, I want to be filled
more and more with Your grace.
I come to Your throne of grace,

mercy and peace in order to
see with Your eyes and be filled
with thanksgiving. I come humbly
asking Your cleansing and liberation,
a fresh new opportunity to be a channel
for Your grace to others. Jesus, be in
my growing in grace.

. . . Speaking the truth in love, we will in all
things grow up into him who is the Head, that
is, Christ. From him the whole body, joined and
held together by every supporting ligament,
grows and builds itself up in love, as each part
does its work.

Ephesians 4:15–16

Mary's Song

And Mary said:

"My soul praises the Lord
  and my spirit rejoices in God my
      Savior,
for he has been mindful
  of the humble state of his serv-
    ant.
From now on all generations will
call me blessed,
  for the Mighty One has done
  great things for me—
    holy is his name.
His mercy extends to those who
fear him,
  from generation to generation.
He has performed mighty deeds
with his arm;
  he has scattered those who are
  proud in their inmost thoughts.
He has brought down rulers from
their thrones
  but has lifted up the humble.

He has filled the hungry with good
things
   but has sent the rich away empty.
He has helped his servant Israel,
   remembering to be merciful
to Abraham and his descendants forever,
   even as he said to our fathers."

Luke 1:46–55